How to Cultivate Mushrooms for Beginners

The Ultimate Guide to Growing Gourmet Fungi Indoors

Kenneth M. Oleary

Table of Content

Introduction

Emma, a keen gardener, discovered a secret treasure one bright day in a charming backyard: a mystery mushroom patch. Her curiosity peaked, and she decided to explore the fascinating field of mushroom farming.

Emma transformed her gardening gloves into amazing instruments for mushroom cultivation with the help of a straightforward manual and unwavering perseverance. Emma discovered the enchanted mysteries of cultivating her mushroom feast, step by step, from selecting the appropriate kinds to building the ideal substrate bed.

Days became an adventure loaded with mycelium, and Emma's backyard became a sanctuary of primordial possibilities. Little pinheads appeared like ethereal beings, developing into plump mushrooms that exhibited a joyful wink. Now a mycological maestro, Emma felt the excitement of a harvest as if it were something out of a fantasy book.

Come along with Emma on her wacky excursion into the core of mushroom farming. Uncover the mysteries concealed beneath each fungus friend's cap. Every spore has the potential to yield a wonderful harvest, so you too can go on a journey with a dash of curiosity and a dash of beginner's luck. Greetings from the fascinating world of mushroom farming, where every chapter is an unfinished tale waiting to be told and the commonplace gives rise to the spectacular.

Chapter 1

Understanding Mushrooms

Those mysterious mushrooms are more than just delicious food. It is crucial for anyone starting a mushroom farm to have a basic awareness of these creatures. To prepare the way for a rewarding adventure into mushroom farming, let's first unpack the fundamentals.

What is a mushroom?

The fruiting bodies of fungi and mushrooms are members of a different kingdom from microbes, plants, and animals. As decomposers who recycle nutrients and break down organic materials, they are essential to ecosystems. The portion of the fungus that is visible and that we usually identify as a mushroom is only a small portion of its intricate structure. Generally speaking, mushrooms are made up of a stem that serves as support and a cap that covers the spore-producing organs (gills or pores). The network of thread-like structures known as the mycelium is the vegetative portion of the fungus that is responsible for growth and nutrition absorption. It is hidden within the substrate.

Essentially, mushrooms are the fruiting bodies of fungi, which are a different kingdom from bacteria, plants, and mammals. The part of the fungal structure that is visible is merely the cap and stem; the vegetative growth component is mycelium, which grows through the substrate.

A mushroom's life cycle consists of mycelial growth, germination, spore dissemination, and final mushroom development. Like seeds, spores germinate to produce mycelium, which forms a network that, in the right circumstances, leads to the creation of the visible mushroom.

Comprehending the structure of a mushroom is essential for cultivating it successfully. Every component of the organism is important to its life cycle, from the cap that protects the structures that produce spores to the stem that provide support and the mycelium that is concealed within the substrate.

The growth of mushrooms is greatly influenced by environmental conditions. Their development is influenced by variables like light, temperature, humidity, and substrate composition. Because different species of mushrooms have different preferences, it is important to understand these needs to cultivate mushrooms successfully.

Growing mushrooms is not a project that is best suited for everyone. Novice mushroom hunters should investigate kinds like oysters, shiitake, or white button mushrooms that are appropriate for their skill level. Every species has different needs and traits, so each one must be carefully considered.

To avoid contamination, it is crucial to maintain a sterile atmosphere when cultivating mushrooms. Beginners need to understand how crucial it is to maintain cleanliness at every stage of the procedure—from preparing the substrate to inoculating—to ensure a robust and fruitful mushroom culture.

In the cultivation of mushrooms, patience is a virtue. The entire procedure takes weeks, from inoculation to harvest. For beginners, it is essential to comprehend and accept this timeline as it will help them develop a patient and thorough attention to detail-mindset.

For beginners, mistakes are unavoidable, but they also present excellent teaching moments. Every error offers an opportunity to improve farming methods. A mindset of constant learning and development is essential to effective mushroom cultivation.

Learning about mushrooms essentially entails exploring their morphology, life cycle, ecological requirements, and the complex craft of growing them. Equipped with this understanding, novices can set out on a quest to not only grow mushrooms but also to enjoy the wonderful realm of fungus.

Importance of Mushroom Cultivation

For beginners, mushroom growing is quite important because of its accessibility, nutritional content, and advantages for the environment. Growing mushrooms provides a simple entrance point for individuals who are new to agriculture or are searching for a fulfilling and sustainable pastime.

First of all, their nutritional value is well known. They are rich in protein, fiber, vitamins, and minerals but low in calories and fat. Growing a wholesome food source that can enhance a balanced diet is a satisfying experience. This becomes more important as more and more people look for nutrient-dense, varied diets to improve their overall health.

Moreover, growing mushrooms is a pretty simple process that takes up little room. In contrast to conventional gardening, mushroom cultivation can be done indoors, providing a viable choice for people with little outside space. Because the culture procedure is so straightforward—straw or sawdust are common substrate materials—beginners may understand the fundamentals of cultivation without having to deal with the complications that come with growing many other types of crops.

The rate at which mushrooms mature is another attractive feature for beginners. Mushrooms can be harvested in a few weeks to a few months, depending on the species. Compared to other crops, this fast-growing cycle gives a sense of accomplishment and speedier results, which inspires passion and confidence in their cultivating abilities.

Furthermore, growing mushrooms encourages sustainability. Mushrooms are effective decomposers, transforming organic materials into beneficial nutrients. Beginners can take advantage of this ecological function to recycle industrial and agricultural waste into rich substrates for mushroom growing, such as wood byproducts or straws. This adds to a circular and sustainable farming method in addition to lowering waste.

Mushrooms are a possible source of money for those new to the economics of farming. Beginners have the chance to convert their passion into a small-scale business because local markets and restaurants are in demand for oyster mushrooms, shiitake, and other gourmet kinds. This economic component provides a useful incentive for individuals hoping to profit monetarily from their gardening endeavors.

Furthermore, growing mushrooms improve the condition of the soil. Enzymes that mushrooms emit during growth break down complex organic substances, adding nutrients to the soil. If beginners choose to pursue more agricultural endeavors, this enhances the soil's general health and fosters better-growing conditions for other crops.

Chapter 2

Getting Started

Growing mushrooms is a fascinating and fulfilling hobby that is becoming more and more popular among connoisseurs and future farmers. Whether you're an enthusiast hoping to grow mushrooms for your use or an enterprising person considering the possibility of starting a mushroom cultivation business, the process of getting started demands thoughtful thought and close attention to detail.

Selecting the appropriate species of mushrooms for growing is crucial. Since each type of mushroom has different growing conditions, beginners can usually succeed with species like oysters, shiitake, or white button mushrooms. When choosing, take into account elements like the local climate, the amount of space you have available, and your tastes.

Establishing a good growing environment is the next stage after selecting the species of mushrooms. Under regulated circumstances that resemble their natural habitat, mushrooms flourish. To provide the mushrooms with a nutrient-rich media to colonize, prepare a growth substrate. A variety of organic materials, such as vermiculite, wood chips, and straw, are used as common substrates. It is essential to properly sterilize the substrate to get rid of any competing organisms that can prevent mushrooms from growing.

You must inoculate the substrate with mushroom spawn after it has been prepared. As the "seed" for growing mushrooms, spawn can be produced from a previous successful batch or purchased from reliable sources. Make sure that the spawn is well distributed over the substrate by handling it with care. The mycelium, which is the thread-like network of mushroom cells, spreads and establishes itself throughout this period, which usually takes a few weeks.

When the substrate is completely colonized, fruiting can be induced. This entails establishing circumstances that promote the growth of fruiting bodies in mushrooms. Change the light, humidity, and temperature to mimic the seasons and let the mycelium know when it's time to start producing mushrooms.

The first indications of mushroom pins may not appear for several weeks, therefore patience is required during this phase.

It is vital to keep growing conditions as ideal as possible during the fruiting period. To maintain appropriate air exchange and avoid carbon dioxide accumulation, adequate ventilation is crucial. Monitor temperature variations to replicate the natural environment and adjust humidity levels to encourage healthy mushroom development.

To avoid contamination in later batches, it's critical to clean and disinfect the growing area after harvest. Consider composting or repurposing leftover substrate as a substrate for future crops, and dispose of it sustainably.

As you get more expertise growing mushrooms, you might investigate more complex methods like cloning, which is copying strains that have proven successful, or experimenting with other substrates to improve flavor and nutritional value. Joining a mushroom enthusiast group can also offer helpful advice, hints for solving problems, and a sense of support.

Necessary Requirements and Supplies

The intriguing process of growing mushrooms requires accuracy and close attention to detail. Cultivators must attend to certain essential criteria that support the general well-being and growth of mushrooms to guarantee a successful harvest.

Substrate: Choosing the right substrate is essential for growing mushrooms. It acts as the mycelium's (the fungus's vegetative portion) growing medium. Blends of organic materials including straw, wood chips, and grains are common substrates. The particular type of mushroom being grown determines the nature of the substrate.

Spores or Culture: Harvesting spores or cultures of the target species of mushrooms is the first step in the mushroom cultivation process. While spores are microscopic reproductive cells, a culture entails moving the fungal network, or mycelium, to a new substrate. The success of the cultivation procedure is largely dependent on the caliber and purity of the spores or culture.

Sterilization Tools: When growing mushrooms, contamination is a continual risk. To maintain a sterile environment, sterilization tools like autoclaves and pressure cookers are essential. It is essential to properly sanitize substrates, containers, and instruments to keep undesired microorganisms from competing with the mycelium of the mushroom.

Containers: Mycelium colonization and subsequent fruiting require an environment that is conducive to mushroom cultivation. They must be proportioned correctly for the selected growing technique, sturdy, and hygienic. Commonly used containers for mushrooms include jars, trays, or plastic bags, depending on the type of mushroom.

Growing Conditions: Developing the ideal growing conditions is crucial to the productive cultivation of mushrooms. Temperature, humidity, and exposure to light are examples of essential factors. Because different species of mushrooms have different preferences for certain environments, these factors must be carefully considered at every stage of the cultivation process.

Ventilation System: For the best possible mushroom development, there must be sufficient air exchange. An efficient ventilation system makes sure that oxygen is replenished and assists in removing carbon dioxide created during mycelium growth. This is especially crucial while the mushrooms are fruiting since they need more airflow.

Watering System: Sufficient moisture levels must be maintained to successfully cultivate mushrooms. A dependable irrigation system—manual or automatic—assists in reaching and maintaining the necessary humidity. Sufficient moisture levels keep the substrate from drying out and promote the growth of mycelial organisms.

pH Measurement Tools: For best growth, mushrooms may have particular pH preferences. The acidity or alkalinity of the substrate can be monitored and adjusted with the use of pH meters or test kits. Sustaining the proper pH balance guarantees a conducive atmosphere for the growth of mushrooms.

Lighting: Although certain species of mushrooms benefit from exposure to light during the fruiting stage, others do not require light throughout the vegetative growth stage. Proper lighting, either artificial or natural, can affect when and how well mushrooms fruit. Achieving the best outcomes requires an understanding of the chosen mushroom species' light requirements.

Clean workstation: To avoid infection, it's critical to keep your workstation tidy and committed.

Frequent hand, tool, and surface sanitization reduces the possibility of unwelcome bacteria entering the cultivation environment. An organized workspace goes a long way toward making the cultivating process successful as a whole.

Creating the Ideal Growing Environment

Establishing a perfect growing environment is essential to growing mushrooms successfully. As distinct creatures, mushrooms have diverse environmental needs at different phases of their life cycles. Cultivators need to carefully evaluate several aspects that contribute to an optimal environment to maximize growth and guarantee a plentiful yield.

Temperature Control: One of the most important variables affecting the growth of mushrooms is temperature. Because different kinds of mushrooms have different preferred temperatures, it's important to keep the chosen species within its proper range. For instance, a warmer temperature is generally needed during the mycelium growth phase, whereas a cooler environment could be required during the fruiting stage. Maintaining a steady temperature is essential to shielding the mushrooms from stress and encouraging their healthy growth.

Controlling Humidity: High humidity conditions are ideal for mushrooms, especially in the early phases of growth. For many types of mushrooms, humidity levels should be kept between 90 and 95 percent normal. This high relative humidity promotes the growth of mycelium and helps to generate primordia, which are tiny pin-shaped mushrooms that eventually become complete fruiting bodies. To keep the mushrooms from drying out too soon during the fruiting period, humidity regulation is especially important.

Ventilation System: Sufficient ventilation is necessary to maintain a constant flow of air, which replenishes oxygen and aids in the removal of carbon dioxide created during mycelium growth. All phases of cultivation require proper ventilation, but during the fruiting period, when mushrooms need more air circulation for optimal development, it becomes even more important. Hazardous gas accumulation is avoided and air quality is maintained with the aid of a well-designed ventilation system.

Lighting Considerations: Although mushrooms do not need light to thrive in their first vegetative stage, during the fruiting stage, some species benefit from exposure to light. Light directs the growth of mushrooms and promotes the production of primordia. You can use low-intensity artificial light or natural light, but the time and intensity should match the requirements of the particular variety of mushrooms you have chosen.

Control of Substrate Moisture: Proper substrate moisture maintenance is necessary for productive mushroom growing. Enough water should be present in the substrate to allow mycelium growth without becoming soggy. The best circumstances for mycelial colonization and subsequent fruiting are created by routinely monitoring and adjusting the substrate moisture levels, frequently with the use of misting or watering devices.

Management of pH Level: The substrate's pH level has a big impact on the growth of mushrooms. Many kinds of mushrooms have preferred pH values, and keeping the pH range within the proper range is essential for mycelial health and nutrient availability. Cultivators can alter and maintain the ideal pH level during the cultivation process with the aid of pH meters or test kits, which can be used for routine monitoring.

Hygiene and Sterility: Successful mushroom production depends on the upkeep of a clean and sterile environment. Efforts can be readily thwarted by contamination, which can result in low yields or total crop failure. The risk of introducing undesired microbes that could damage or compete with the mushroom mycelium is reduced by routinely sanitizing tools, equipment, and the production environment.

Monitoring and Modifications: It is crucial to regularly check the substrate conditions, temperature, humidity, and other environmental factors. Growers need to be ready to modify their practices in response to the particular needs of the species of mushrooms they are growing. Timely interventions and adjustments are made possible by keeping meticulous records and paying attention to the small changes in the growth environment.

Chapter 3

Choosing the Right Mushroom Species

Choosing the proper species of mushrooms to cultivate is an important step that will have a big impact on the success of your venture. There are differences in the market demand, growing needs, and preferred environments for different types of mushrooms. Here are some steps to help you select the best species of mushrooms for your gardening endeavor.

- **Market Demand:** Take into account the demand for different mushroom species on the market before getting too far into the details of growing. Making an informed decision is aided by knowing customer preferences in your target market or location. Although popular options like portobellos, shiitake, button mushrooms, and oyster mushrooms are frequently in great demand, market dynamics can also be influenced by regional tastes and culinary trends.

- **Cultivation Expertise:** Assess your knowledge and experience in cultivation. While some mushrooms need a more advanced skill set, others are more forgiving to beginners. Because they are resilient to environmental changes and have a very simple production technique, oyster mushrooms are frequently suggested for beginning farmers. More seasoned growers might investigate cultivators that are more suited to certain types, such as maitake or shiitake.

- **Environmental Factors:** Certain environmental factors are favorable to the growth of different types of mushrooms. Think about things like the needed amount of light, humidity, and temperature. For instance, oyster mushrooms can thrive in reduced light levels and can withstand a wide range of temperatures, making them tolerant of a variety of environmental situations. Conversely, shiitake mushrooms require a more regulated and colder environment.

- **Growing Substrate:** The type of mushroom being grown has a big influence on the growing substrate selection. While some mushrooms, like shiitake, are best grown on substrates based on hardwood, others, like lion's mane, may grow on a wide range of substrates, including straw and agricultural waste. Take into account the cost and accessibility of appropriate substrates when selecting a type of mushroom.

- **Timeline for Cultivation:** The time required for the cultivation of various mushroom species varies. Certain mushrooms are good for shorter turnaround times since they may be harvested in a matter of weeks, such as oyster mushrooms, which grow quickly. Species such as shiitake, on the other hand, could have a longer cultivation cycle and hence need more time and preparation.

- **Space and Equipment:** Assess the space and cultivation-related equipment you have at your disposal. Oysters are one type of mushroom that grows well in home or small-scale environments. Larger mushrooms, such as maitake, or more intricate types could call for larger growing spaces and specialized equipment.

- **Personal Preferences and Objectives:** Take into account your objectives and preferences when it comes to growing mushrooms. Are you searching for a certain type of food, something medicinal, or just large yields? You can find a mushroom species that shares your interests and aspirations by following your preferences and aims.

- **Availability of Spores or Culture:** Verify that the chosen mushroom species' spores or culture can be easily obtained. The availability of high-quality spores or a dependable culture is essential to the accomplishment of your growing endeavor. Look into reliable vendors and their availability in your area.

- **Risk management:** Assess the possible risks connected to each type of mushroom. Certain types need closer observation and care since they are more prone to illnesses or pests. By being aware of the dangers, you may take preventative action and lessen the possibility that problems will negatively impact your harvest.

Popular Varieties

There is a vast array of mushroom kinds available for cultivation, each with distinct qualities, tastes, and needs for growth. Popular kinds are frequently selected by growers according to criteria like consumer demand, ease of cultivation, and individual preferences. An examination of a few commonly grown mushroom types is provided below:

- **Shiitake (Lentinula edodes):** One of the most well-liked and extensively grown types of mushrooms worldwide. Shiitake mushrooms are well-known for their meaty texture and deep, umami flavor. They are also very useful in cooking. Usually, these mushrooms are found growing on hardwood logs or substrates enriched with sawdust. Growing shiitake mushrooms calls for particular climatic parameters, such as regulated humidity and colder temperatures. Shiitake mushrooms are used extensively in both traditional medicine and cooking due to their supposed medicinal qualities.

- **Oyster (Pleurotus spp.):** Oyster mushrooms are prized for their velvety texture and subtle flavor. They are available in a variety of hues, including pink, yellow, and white. Because of their extreme adaptability, oysters may grow on a wide range of substrates, such as wood chips, straw, and agricultural waste. They are a great option for both inexperienced and seasoned growers due to their quick development and tolerance to a wide temperature range. From stir-fries to soups, oyster mushrooms are frequently utilized in a variety of culinary preparations.

- **Button (Agaricus bisporus):** Often referred to as white mushrooms, button mushrooms are arguably the most well-known type that can be purchased in stores. Their firm texture and mild flavor make them ideal for a variety of culinary applications. Button mushrooms grow well on both small- and large-scale substrates and are typically grown on composted materials. This variety contains a range of maturity stages; the youngest are buttons, while the more mature forms of the same species are represented by cremini or portobello mushrooms.

- **Maitake (Grifola frondosa):** Known as the "hen of the words" it has a strong, earthy flavor and a distinctive, frilly look. Maitake mushrooms are utilized in both culinary and medicinal contexts, and they are frequently sought after for their possible health advantages. Usually, cultivation entails growing them on hardwood sawdust blocks treated with nutrients. Maitakes are a valuable addition to the arsenal of mushroom cultivators due to their distinct taste and possible therapeutic benefits, even though they may require a longer culture cycle.

- **Lion's Mane (Hericium erinaceus):** These are well-known for having a unique appearance that mimics dripping white icicles. Lion's mane has become more and more popular in vegetarian and vegan cooking due to its gentle marine flavor. They are frequently grown on sawdust blocks treated with nutrients. Lion's mane mushrooms are popular due to their possible neurological and cognitive benefits, which go beyond their culinary usage.

- **Enoki (Flammulina velutipes):** They are distinguished by their thin caps and long, slender stems. Enoki mushrooms have a gentle, somewhat crunchy texture and are often used in Asian salads and soups. Growing them at lower temperatures, frequently on a substrate of wheat straw or other such materials, is the process of cultivation. Both professionals and home cooks adore them for their distinctive look and delicate flavor.

- **Shimeji (Hypsizygus tessellatus):** They are available in a variety of hues, including brown and white. Their texture is firm and slightly chewy, and they have a nutty flavor. Grain or wood chips are commonly used as a substrate for Shimejis cultivation. Their unique look and adaptability in the kitchen, especially when making Asian cuisine, add to their appeal to growers.

Chapter 4

Mushroom Life Cycle

Mushrooms have a fascinating life cycle that mimics the seasonal dance in the enchanted world of gardens. The modest spore, a little seed-like object carried by the wind, is where this amazing trip starts.

These spores, each perhaps a sign of life, find their way to appropriate habitats when the light wind blows across the flower beds. The spore cradles the promise of a new mushroom, whether it is perched on decomposing debris in the garden or nestled in the soil. It waits patiently for the ideal circumstances before acting.

The spore starts its journey through a metamorphosis when the conditions in the garden come together in a balanced dance of moisture, warmth, and nutrients. The enchanted subterranean network known as mycelium appears in the calm crevices of the garden soil. This structure resembles a web that weaves across the substrate, secreting enzymes that decompose organic debris, and acting as a quiet gardener, preparing the soil for the mushroom to grow.

The primordia, the great sight, are put in motion by the ceaseless expansion of mycelium. These are little, mushroom-like forms that resemble buds and are ready to open. It's a delicate moment, the change from the great overture of the mushroom's premiere to the secret underground ballet.

The mushroom top gives off a burst of energy and reaches upward, defying gravity to reach the sunshine in the garden. Beneath the cap, a maze of complex passageways known as Gills opens up, providing spores with a means of escape into the world of the garden. The cap, which is frequently decorated in a variety of hues, is evidence of the wacky diversity that can be discovered in the fungus-filled garden.

Now when it has fully grown, the mushroom stands tall and becomes a symbol of life in the garden. However, this is only a brief chapter in the cyclical story; it is not the end. The mushroom ages as time stitches its tapestry together. The circle of life is continued as its once-tense and colorful cap begins to wither and release spores into the garden wind.

The mushroom eventually bows out gracefully, sinking back into the garden soil from which it originated. As it breaks down, it leaves behind vital nutrients that the garden needs to support the next round of flowers and veggies. Constantly alert, the mycelium continues to grow underground in the garden, threading its silent threads through the organic garden bed's tapestry.

Thus, in the beloved haven of the garden, the life cycle of mushrooms continues—a symphony of growth, decay, and rebirth orchestrated by the invisible hands of nature. Every mushroom, a transient star in this garden drama, adds to the complex ecology of the area and is a small player in the vast play of life.

From Spore to Harvest

Small spores are the first stage of mushroom growth. Similar to seeds, these spores are cultured on a particular medium, like an agar plate that is loaded with nutrients. Once established, they begin to grow mycelium, which is tiny threads. This phase, which prepares the soil for mushrooms, is comparable to a plant's roots.

The mycelium develops into tiny lumps known as primordia. These are the first indications of impending mushroom growth. Through meticulous regulation of variables like temperature and humidity, these primordial forms develop into tiny fungi called pins. This is an important stage where good care is necessary to guarantee mushroom growth.

It's time to harvest when these pins turn into fully formed mushrooms. Harvesting entails selecting the mature mushrooms with care. For the producers, this is a moment of great satisfaction because the mushrooms have grown from microscopic spores.

But that's not where the narrative ends. When the correct circumstances arise, the mycelium that is still present in the growing medium is prepared to restart the cycle. Growth, harvest, and regrowth are all part of this ongoing cycle.

Growing mushrooms is not only about harvesting them; sustainability is also important. The mycelium-enriched residual material from the mushroom growth can be used again as a soil enhancer. Fields and gardens get fertility from this recycling.

Growers take on the role of caregivers in the realm of mushroom growing, ensuring that all the necessary circumstances are met for a successful harvest. It's a voyage that requires endurance, focus, and consideration for the fungal natural processes. The process of growing mushrooms, from microscopic spores to an abundant harvest, is a lovely collaboration between human labor and the amazing realm of fungi.

Understanding Growth Stages

The process of growing mushrooms is an intriguing one that involves several growth stages. Each of these stages has a specific importance in the life cycle of the mushroom and is essential for successful cultivation. The following five salient features clarify these developmental phases:

Inoculation: The process of cultivating mushrooms starts with inoculation. At this point, the growth process is initiated by introducing spores or mycelium onto a substrate. It's similar to sowing seeds, with the selected substrate being essential in supplying the nutrients required for mycelium growth.

Colonization: Mycelium spreads and colonizes the substrate at this crucial phase. The development of a white, web-like network known as the mycelial mat is what defines this stage. During colonization, patience is essential because it lays the groundwork for healthy mushroom growth. The temperature and nature of the substrate have a big impact on how quickly colonies spread.

Primordia Formation: Once the mycelium has finished colonizing, small pinhead-sized structures called primordia start to take shape. This is when vegetative growth ends and reproductive growth begins. At this point, humidity levels and the exchange of fresh air become crucial variables. The mushroom caps that will eventually emerge are represented by the primordia, which frequently resemble little bumps.

Development of Fruiting Bodies: From the primordia, fruiting bodies, or mushrooms, arise. Enough environmental conditions are essential for the development of healthy, well-formed mushrooms during this stage. A delicate dance is performed by variables like temperature, humidity, and light exposure to determine the final harvest's size and quality.

Harvesting: The process of growing mushrooms comes to an end with harvesting. Right now, timing is crucial. If the mushrooms are harvested too soon, they may not have grown to their full potential; if they are harvested too late, they may release spores that could harm subsequent harvests. Careful harvesting methods aid in maintaining the mycelial network for possible future flushes.

Gaining proficiency in these growth phases is essential for a fruitful endeavor involving mushroom farming. Every step necessitates meticulous attention to detail, from creating the ideal atmosphere to guaranteeing appropriate hygiene procedures. Understanding the subtleties of each stage allows growers to fine-

tune their techniques and produce abundant
and superior yields of mushrooms.

Chapter 5

Common Challenges and Solutions

Some common challenges include:

1. Contamination

Challenge: The challenge lies in the unwanted bacteria, molds, or other fungi vying for the mycelium of the mushroom.

Solution: From substrate preparation to inoculation, maintain a high standard of cleanliness at all times. Work in a sterile, controlled atmosphere and follow the correct sterilizing procedures.

2. Gradual Colonization

Challenge: The mycelium is taking longer than usual to cover the substrate completely.

Solution: Make sure the surroundings are ideal, with the right humidity and temperature.

Examine the substrate's quality and make any required adjustments.

3. Poor Fruiting Body Formation

Challenge: improperly formed mushrooms that have asymmetrical forms or inhibited growth.

Solution: Modify the lighting, humidity, and fresh air exchange in the surrounding area. Verify the nutritional value of the substrate and make any required adjustments.

4. Low Yield of Mushrooms

Challenge: Harvests falling short of anticipated yields.

Solution: Examine and improve cultivation characteristics such as moisture content, substrate composition, and surrounding circumstances. Make sure you pick mature mushrooms at the right time.

5. Pests or Fungus Gnats:

Challenge: Mycelium-damaging pest infestation, such as fungus gnats.

Solution: The cultivation space should be kept tidy and well-sealed. Use natural predators like nematodes or sticky traps as pest control techniques.

6. Uneven Pinning:

Challenge: Pinheads form unevenly over the substrate.

Solution: Make sure that all fruiting conditions are consistent, including light exposure and air exchange with fresh air. Turn over or reposition the growing containers.

7. Overhydration or Dehydration:

Challenge: The excessive moisture or dryness of the mushrooms hinders their growth.

Solution: Keep an eye on humidity levels and modify them as necessary. If the substrate is too dry, spray it and make sure to properly drain any extra water. A balanced moisture content must be maintained for the optimal growth of mushrooms.

It takes a combination of diligence, attention to detail, and flexibility to overcome these typical obstacles. A more successful growth experience can be achieved by keeping a close eye on the growing environment, maintaining proper hygiene, and making adjustments according to the unique requirements of your species of mushrooms.

Dealing With Contamination

A constant concern in the cultivation of mushrooms is contamination, which necessitates quick corrective action and vigilance. To prevent undesirable germs, molds, or rival fungi from invading, growers must keep their surroundings sterile and clean. Here are some steps to handling contamination in the mushroom farming industry:

1. Sterilization as a Prevention Measure:

Key Practice: Start by thoroughly sterilizing all tools and supplies used in the growing procedure. Substrates, receptacles, and any instruments used for inoculation fall under this category.

Methodical Approach: For complete sterilization, use autoclaves or pressure cookers. Observe the suggested time and temperature ranges for the particular items you are handling.

2. Using Aseptic Methods During Inoculation:

Key Practice: When adding spores or mycelium to the substrate, use aseptic methods. This crucial phase is when contamination frequently happens.

Methodical Approach: Operate in a hygienic and well-regulated setting. If a laminar flow hood is available, use it; if not, establish an improvised clean area with little to no air disturbance. Use flame-sterilized instruments, put on sterile gloves, and refrain from making needless movements that could spread pollutants.

3. Track and Spot Early Warning Signs:

Key Practice: As the mycelium colonizes, keep an eye out for any indications of contamination in the growth substrate.

Methodical Approach: Keep an eye out for any discoloration, bad smells, or odd growth patterns. Spots, patches, or color changes in the mycelial tissue can be signs of contamination. To stop deviations from spreading further, deal with them immediately.

4. Isolate Affected Areas:

Key Practice: To stop undesired bacteria from spreading, isolate infected areas.

Methodical Approach: Immediately remove the contaminated area from the substrate if contamination is found. To prevent additional contamination inside the crop area,

dispose of the contaminated item
appropriately.

5. Modify the surrounding environment:

Key Practice: Establish conditions that promote the growth of mushrooms over other pollutants.

Methodical Approach: Make sure the humidity and temperature are just right for mycelial growth. It is common for contaminants to flourish in environments that are not ideal for the targeted species of mushrooms.

6. Put Air Filtration in Place:

Key Practice: Installing air filtration systems to reduce the amount of airborne contaminants introduced.

Methodical Approach: To capture airborne particles, place HEPA filters in the cultivation area. Keep the growth area clean and tightly sealed to minimize the chance of outside pollutants getting in.

7. Isolate Emerging Cultures:

Key Practice: Before bringing new spore syringes or cultures into the main cultivation area, quarantine them.

Methodical Approach: Vaccinate a small batch individually and keep an eye out for any contamination symptoms. Proceed to inoculate the main cultivation area if the quarantine batch proves to be clean.

8. Maintain Tight Hygiene:

Key Practice: To reduce the chance of introducing pollutants, enforce strict personal and workplace hygiene.

Methodical Approach: Before touching any cultivation materials, properly wash your hands. When entering the cultivation space, make sure your attire is clean and acceptable. You may also want to use a disinfection footbath.

9. Ongoing Education and Adjustment:

Key Practice: Foster an attitude of constant adaptability and development.

Methodical Approach: Keep yourself informed on fresh contamination threats and cutting-edge precautions regularly. Keep up with developments in cultivation methods and sterilization procedures.

It is possible to successfully fight contamination and create the conditions for a healthy harvest free of contamination by including these focused and exact techniques in your mushroom growing regimen. Recall that the secret to effective mushroom gardening is to be both proactive and watchful.

Health Benefits of Mushrooms

Though their nutritional significance is sometimes overlooked, mushrooms are a wonderful addition to any diet because of their many health advantages. It's important to comprehend the health benefits of mushrooms as you explore the intriguing world of mushroom farming.

Brimming with Nutrients: Packed with vital vitamins and minerals, mushrooms are a nutrient-dense food. Especially important for energy metabolism and general health, they are especially high in B vitamins including pantothenic acid, niacin, and riboflavin.

Support for the Immune System: Some types of mushrooms, such as shiitake and maitake, have been shown to include beta-glucans, which have been connected to improved immunity. These substances aid in the body's defense against infections and diseases by boosting the immune system.

Antioxidant Properties: The antioxidant properties of mushrooms, such as ergothioneine and selenium, make them a powerful source of antioxidants. By counteracting the damaging effects of free radicals, these antioxidants lower the body's risk of oxidative stress and chronic illnesses.

Cardiovascular Health: Eating mushrooms regularly has been linked to improved heart health. They contain substances like fiber and beta-glucans that help lower cholesterol, support heart health and lower the risk of cardiovascular illnesses.

Blood Sugar Regulation: Reishi and other mushrooms may be involved in blood sugar regulation. These mushrooms' constituents may improve insulin sensitivity, which makes them advantageous for people who already have diabetes or are at risk of getting it.

Anti-Inflammatory Effects: Bioactive substances found in mushrooms have anti-inflammatory qualities. For those with inflammatory diseases, this might be very helpful as it helps to reduce inflammation and related symptoms.

Vitamin D Synthesis: Some types of mushrooms can produce vitamin D on their own when exposed to sunshine. For strong bones, a healthy immune system, and general well-being, this vitamin is essential. Including these mushrooms in your growing process can offer a free-radical vitamin D source.

Nutritional Value

In addition to being praised for their distinct tastes and textures, mushrooms have a wide range of nutritional advantages. Understanding the rich nutritional composition of these fungi becomes crucial as you venture deeper into the world of mushroom growing.

1. Low in Calories, High in Nutrients: Being low in calories, mushrooms are a great meal option for anyone trying to control their weight. Mushrooms are low in calories but high in nutrients, offering a wide range of vitamins and minerals.

2. Rich in Minerals: Selenium, copper, potassium, and phosphorus are just a few of the vital elements found in mushrooms. Specifically, selenium is an antioxidant mineral that supports immunological function and shields cells from oxidative damage.

3. Protein Content: Mushrooms provide a significant amount of protein, but not as much as animal goods. They are therefore a beneficial supplement to vegetarian and vegan diets. As a complete protein source, mushrooms provide all of the essential amino acids found in protein.

4. Dietary Fiber for Digestive Health:

Rich in dietary fiber, mushrooms help support digestive health. Constipation is avoided, gut health is preserved, and general digestive function is supported by fiber.

5. Low in Sodium and Saturated Fat:

Mushrooms are a heart-healthy dietary option since they are naturally low in sodium and saturated fat. You can lower your risk of cardiovascular disease and maintain healthy blood pressure by including mushrooms in your diet.

6. Bioactive substances:

Polysaccharides and beta-glucans are two examples of the bioactive substances found in mushrooms. Numerous health benefits, including immune system regulation and possible anti-cancer effects, have been associated with these substances.

7. Versatility in Culinary Applications:

Mushrooms provide food depth and umami flavor in addition to their nutritious advantages. These are adaptable ingredients that work well in a variety of dishes, including salads, main meals, soups, and stir-fries.

Mushrooms have much more nutritional worth than only their flavor and texture. Growing your mushrooms at home can be a great way to add a variety of vital nutrients to your diet and improve your general health and well-being.

Potential Medicinal Properties

Mushrooms offer a fascinating investigation of the possible therapeutic qualities present in a variety of mushroom species, in addition to culinary adventure.

1. Immune System Modulation: The immune system is stimulated and regulated by active substances such as beta-glucans, which improve the immune system's response to infections and illnesses.

2. Adaptogenic Properties: Materials known as adaptogens aid the body in adjusting to stress. As adaptogenic mushrooms, reishi and cordyceps are known to help manage both physical and emotional stressors, possibly fostering resilience and balance.

3. Antimicrobial and Antibacterial Effects: Certain mushrooms can fight off bacteria and germs. For example, lentinan, a substance found in shiitake mushrooms, may have antiviral and antibacterial properties that support the body's fight against infections.

4. Potential to Fight Cancer: Studies indicate that mushrooms might be able to fight cancer. Cancer research is interested in compounds found in many mushrooms, such as beta-glucans, polysaccharides, and lectins, which may have anti-tumor properties.

5. Blood Sugar Regulation: Research has been done on the effects of certain mushrooms, like maitake, on blood sugar regulation. Active ingredients may improve insulin sensitivity, which could be advantageous for those with diabetes or those who are at risk of getting the disease.

6. Neuroprotective Effects: The neuroprotective qualities of several mushrooms, such as Lion's Mane (Hericium erinaceus), have been studied. These mushrooms contain compounds that may promote the synthesis of nerve growth factor (NGF), which may aid in nerve regeneration and cognitive function.

7. Anti-Allergic Properties: The possibility of anti-allergic effects from compounds present in mushrooms such as Agaricus bisporus has been investigated. These could lessen the intensity of allergy reactions by regulating immunological responses.

Chapter 6

Identifying Poisonous Mushrooms

To protect cultivators and customers alike, recognizing toxic mushrooms is an essential part of the mushroom-growing process. While growing mushrooms is a fulfilling activity, it is important to know which kinds are harmful and which are edible.

1. Knowledge of the Species: A thorough grasp of the species being farmed is the first step towards successful mushroom growth. Different species of mushrooms have unique traits, development habits, and above all varying degrees of toxicity. To reduce their chance of growing toxic types, aspiring cultivators should educate themselves about the particular mushrooms they intend to cultivate.

2. Morphological Features: Identification of mushrooms requires a review of their morphological characteristics. Crucial hints can be found in characteristics including stem structure, gill attachment, color, and shape of the cap. Poisonous mushrooms frequently have distinctive visual characteristics, such as caps with vivid colors or patterns. To spot any abnormalities, a cultivator needs to closely monitor these characteristics during the growth stages.

3. Spore Print Analysis: Spore print analysis is an additional technique for mushroom identification. In essence, the color of the mushroom's expelled spores is represented by the spore print. A grown mushroom cap can be placed on paper so that the fungus can release spores. The resulting spore print can be identified and used to distinguish between edible and deadly kinds by comparing them to trustworthy references.

4. Mycotoxin Testing: Cultivators can use mycotoxin testing as a more scientific method. Certain fungi create dangerous chemicals called mycotoxins, which can be found in some poisonous mushrooms. Mycotoxin testing on cultured mushrooms adds another level of security by giving a numerical representation of possible toxicity.

5. Expert Consultation: Speaking with knowledgeable mycologists or cultivators of mushrooms is a great resource. These people are quite knowledgeable and can provide advice on correctly identifying mushrooms. One way to connect mushroom cultivators with a community of professionals willing to exchange knowledge and insights is to join local mushroom clubs, go to workshops, or participate in online forums.

6. Growth Environment Observation:

It's important to comprehend the conditions in which mushrooms grow. Certain deadly mushrooms only grow in particular environments or circumstances. Potential hazards can be identified by keeping an eye on the farmed mushrooms' natural environment and growing circumstances. This involves keeping an eye out for any indications of contamination or anomalies in the growing procedure.

7. Constant Learning and Updates:

Mycology is a dynamic science where discoveries and classifications are made as a result of continuing research. Growers have to remain up-to-date on the most recent advancements in the classification and identification of mushrooms. Updating knowledge regularly guarantees that mushroom growers have access to the most recent data, enabling them to make well-informed decisions regarding their harvests.

Warning Signs and Dangers

Identifying poisonous mushrooms requires a keen understanding of warning signs and potential dangers. Mushroom enthusiasts and cultivators alike must be aware of specific indicators that differentiate toxic varieties from their edible counterparts.

1. Discoloration and Unusual Colors:

One of the most noticeable warning signs is the presence of vibrant or unusual colors. Many poisonous mushrooms exhibit bright reds, yellows, or blues, serving as a visual cue of potential danger. Edible mushrooms typically have more muted and earthy tones. Cultivators should be wary of any mushroom displaying a striking color palette, especially if it deviates from the expected hues of the species.

2. Foul Odor: A pungent or foul odor can be a strong indicator of toxicity. Edible mushrooms generally have a pleasant, earthy scent. In contrast, poisonous varieties may emit an unpleasant or acrid smell. Cultivators should trust their sense of smell during the identification process and exercise caution if a mushroom has an off-putting aroma.

3. Rapid Bruising or Color Changes:

Some poisonous mushrooms undergo rapid color changes or bruising when touched. Edible mushrooms typically maintain their color and integrity when handled. Observing any immediate alterations in color or the appearance of bruises on the mushroom's flesh should raise concerns about potential toxicity.

4. Inconsistent Growth Patterns:

Healthy mushrooms typically exhibit consistent growth patterns. Deviations such as irregular cap shapes, unusual stem formations, or abnormal gill structures may indicate a poisonous variety. Cultivators should closely monitor the development of mushrooms and be wary of any anomalies that diverge from the expected characteristics of the chosen species.

5. Habitat Warning Signs: The environment in which mushrooms grow can also provide warning signs. Some poisonous mushrooms prefer specific ecosystems or habitats. Cultivators should be cautious if they notice mushrooms growing in areas associated with toxicity, such as near certain tree species or in contaminated soil. Understanding the preferred habitats of different mushrooms contributes to a safer identification process.

6. Lack of Identifiable Features: Edible mushrooms typically have distinct and recognizable features. If a mushroom lacks clear identification characteristics or closely resembles a poisonous species, caution is warranted. In such cases, relying on expert guidance or conducting thorough research becomes crucial to avoid potential dangers.

7. Regional Variations: Mushroom toxicity can vary regionally, and certain areas may be home to unique poisonous species. Cultivators should be aware of the specific mushrooms prevalent in their region and stay informed about any newly discovered toxic varieties. Local mycological expertise and community knowledge are invaluable resources for navigating regional variations in mushroom toxicity.

Safety Measures for Mushroom Foragers

Foragers of mushrooms might find great pleasure in the activity, as can cultivators. But in all the excitement of searching for delicious mushrooms, safety must always come first. Below are some important safety precautions to take when mushroom foraging:

1. Species Identification: Correct species identification is essential to mushroom foraging safety. Gain a thorough awareness of the differences between edible and deadly mushrooms before picking any. To improve your identification abilities, consult dependable field guides, professional guidance, and internet resources.

2. Know Your Local Flora and Fauna:

Distinctive species of mushrooms can be found in different areas. Learn about the local wildlife and plants, as well as the ecosystems that support the growth of mushrooms. This information lessens the possibility of unintentionally gathering harmful mushrooms and helps identify possible threats.

3. Attend Foraging seminars:

Taught by seasoned mycologists, foraging seminars offer priceless advice on how to hunt mushrooms safely. Participants acquire practical experience, pick up identifying skills, and get advice on telling edible from harmful types. These courses improve practical abilities and create a more secure environment for foraging.

4. Make Use of Several Identification Features:

Make use of a variety of identification features, such as stem characteristics, spore color, gill structure, and cap color. By cross-referencing several criteria, you can increase the safety of your foraged mushrooms by lowering the possibility of misidentification.

5. Steer clear of solo foraging:

Foragers should always abide by the maxim "safety in numbers." When possible, go foraging with knowledgeable people or other hobbyists. By pooling expertise, collaborative foraging lowers the possibility of identification errors and ensures a quicker response in an emergency.

6. Carry Essential Tools: Make sure you have the necessary tools, like a magnifying lens for closer examination, a robust basket to allow spores to spread, and a knife for accurate harvesting. With the aid of these tools, you may collect mushrooms more effectively and with less impact on the surrounding area.

7. Protective Gear: To keep safe from ticks, insects, and other potential threats in the foraging area, wear proper clothes, such as long sleeves, long pants, and sturdy boots. To further prevent direct contact with mushrooms and any irritants, think about donning gloves.

8. Remain Hydrated and Nourished:
Extended periods of foraging may be physically taxing. To keep your energy and focus, make sure you eat a healthy diet and stay hydrated. Bring water and some snacks so you can stay energized during the foraging trip.

9. Leave No Trace: When hunting for mushrooms, have a "leave no trace" attitude. Reduce your impact on the environment by not destroying other plants' and mushrooms' habitats. The conservation of ecosystems for future generations is aided by ethical foraging techniques.

10. Emergency Preparedness: Keep a basic first aid kit on hand in case of unanticipated events. Know where the closest hospitals are located, and carry a cell phone or other communication equipment in case of an emergency.

11. Review Local Laws: Make sure you are aware of and abide by any local laws about mushroom foraging. Restrictions may apply in some locations to safeguard particular species or ecosystems. Adhering to these rules

guarantees environmentally responsible
foraging methods and encourages
environmental preservation.

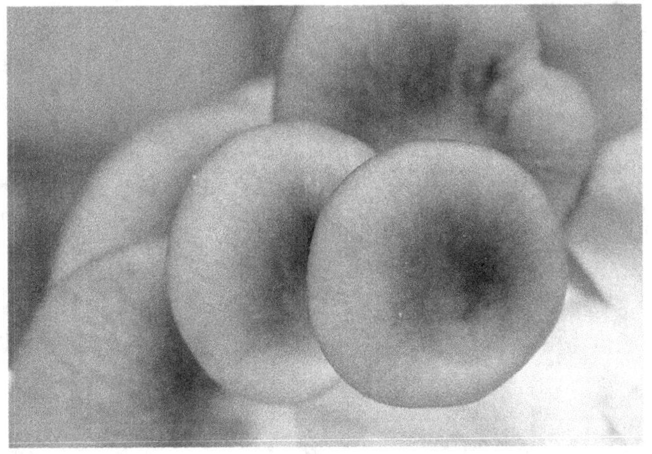

Chapter 7

Harvesting and Storage

To guarantee the quality and durability of your harvest, harvesting, and storage are crucial phases in the mushroom farming process that need to be carefully considered. Time is of the essence when harvesting. The ideal time to harvest mushrooms is right before the cap completely swells, achieving a balance between the undeveloped and spore-releasing stages. To avoid causing too much disturbance to the mycelium network, harvest mushrooms with care. Gently twist or clip the mushrooms off of the substrate.

Additionally, frequency is important. Mature mushrooms should be harvested as soon as possible to encourage the growth of new ones and preserve the ideal growing conditions. Choose clean, sharp equipment, like shears or knives, when using them to avoid contaminating and preserve the integrity of the mushrooms.

Going on to storage, container selection is quite important. To ensure proper ventilation, choose permeable materials like paper bags or perforated plastic. Steer clear of airtight containers as these may cause moisture to accumulate and affect the mushrooms' freshness. For short-term storage, refrigeration is your best bet. Keep mushrooms out of direct sunlight and store them in a paper bag or a vented container in the refrigerator.

This method of drying is dependable for long-term storage. To completely dry the mushrooms, place them in a well-ventilated space or use a food dehydrator. After they have dried, place them in cool, dark places in sealed containers. When dried properly, mushrooms retain their taste for a long time and can be rehydrated for use in cooking.

Regardless of the method used, moisture is the enemy of preserved mushrooms. Before storage, make sure the mushrooms are sufficiently dry to inhibit bacterial growth and spoiling. Perform a quality check before storage, regardless of the storage type you have selected. Examine every mushroom for signs of deterioration, mold, or injury. Remove any weakened specimens to avoid them going bad.

Good mushroom cultivation requires close attention to the details of harvesting and storage. Cultivators can reap the rewards of their mushroom cultivating endeavors when they follow these practices, which range from careful harvesting techniques to considerate storage methods. All of these practices work together to ensure a plentiful and sustainable crop.

Knowing When to Harvest

Knowing when to harvest mushrooms is a crucial aspect of successful cultivation. Harvesting at the right time ensures optimal flavor, texture, and nutritional content. Here is a guide on how to determine the perfect moment to harvest your mushrooms.

1. Observation of Growth Stages:

Mushrooms go through different growth stages. The initial pinning stage is followed by the development of the fruiting body.

Observe the color, size, and shape of the caps. Once the caps have fully opened and the gills are visible, it's usually a sign that the mushrooms are ready for harvest.

2. Veil Break:

The veil is a thin membrane beneath the cap that protects the gills. As the mushroom matures, the veil stretches and eventually breaks.

Harvesting just before or right after the veil break is optimal for many mushroom varieties, as it ensures a firmer texture and better flavor.

3. Spore Release:

Some mushrooms release spores as they mature. Harvesting just before spore release helps avoid a mess and preserves the quality of the remaining mushrooms.

Look for signs of a color change in the spores; this is an indication that the mushrooms are approaching maturity.

4. Cap Expansion:

Monitor the expansion of the mushroom cap. Once it reaches its maximum size and begins to flatten out, it's a good time to harvest.

Delaying the harvest after the cap has fully expanded may lead to a loss of quality, as some mushrooms tend to deteriorate rapidly.

5. Texture and Firmness:

Gently touch the mushrooms to assess their firmness. Mushrooms harvested at the right time will have a taut and robust feel.

Overly mature mushrooms might become mushy or have a slimy texture, affecting both taste and appearance.

6. Cropping Continuously:

For continuous harvest, pick mature mushrooms individually rather than waiting for the entire flush to mature.

This allows younger mushrooms to continue growing, ensuring a steady supply over time.

7. Environmental Factors:

Consider environmental conditions. Changes in humidity, temperature, and light can influence the speed of mushroom development.

Regularly check your cultivation environment and adjust harvesting times accordingly.

8. Species-Specific Considerations:

Different mushroom species have unique characteristics. Some varieties have specific indicators of maturity.

Research the specific requirements of the mushroom species you are cultivating to make informed decisions.

Proper Techniques for Preservation

Harvested mushrooms must be preserved to increase their shelf life and retain quality. The following are some techniques for successfully preserving mushrooms throughout cultivation:

1. Timely Gathering:

To keep mushrooms fresh and avoid overripening, harvest them quickly.

2. Trash Removal and Pruning:

Clean mushrooms gently to get rid of dirt, and cut off stems to stop germs from growing.

3. Prevent Waterlogging:

Reduce the amount of water exposed to avoid moisture absorption; pat dry if necessary.

4. Refrigeration:

Keep mushrooms chilled between 32 and 38 degrees Fahrenheit in a ventilated container.

5. Dehydration:

To prolong the shelf life of mushrooms, slice and dehydrate them; rehydrate as required.

6. Freezing:

Sliced mushrooms work best when frozen in advance on a tray; use them in prepared meals.

7. Pickling:

For a tangy flavor, soak cleaned mushrooms in a mixture of vinegar, water, and salt.

8. Canning:

Follow canning instructions to preserve mushrooms in jars with water, salt, and/or vinegar.

9. Infusion of Oil:

To preserve mushrooms in a tasty way, sauté them and store them in oil.

10. Using Citric Acid:

To keep food from browning and to make it look better, squeeze in some lemon juice.

Conclusion

In conclusion, "How to Grow Mushrooms for Beginners" is a guide that introduces beginners to the exciting realm of mushroom farming. Readers will learn about the nuances of choosing the correct species, setting up the perfect growing environment, and raising mycelium to fruition as they turn the pages. Not only does the book provide instructions, but it also gives enthusiasts the know-how to grow a wide range of mushrooms at home.

Simplifying the procedure fosters competence and self-assurance. As the final chapter closes, readers are not just equipped with practical skills but a newfound appreciation for the delicate balance required to coax fungi from spore to harvest. Whether pursuing this as a hobby or seeking sustainable, homegrown alternatives, "How to Grow Mushrooms for Beginners" leaves readers inspired and ready to embark on their mycological adventures.

We appreciate your time spent reading through "How to Grow Mushrooms for Beginners." I hope that this book has provided valuable insight and practical knowledge on growing mushrooms. We sincerely appreciate your interest in this topic and your inquiry. Recall that your investigation into the broad and fascinating world of mushrooms is the first step in an enlightening journey.

Happy Growing!!

Bonus

Medical Mushrooms to Boost Your Health

- Reishi (Ganoderma lucidum): Known for immune support.
- Chaga (Inonotus obliquus): Rich in antioxidants.
- Cordyceps (Cordyceps militaris): Enhances stamina and energy.
- Lion's Mane (Hericium erinaceus): Supports cognitive function.
- Turkey Tail (Trametes versicolor): Immune-modulating properties.
- Shiitake (Lentinula edodes): Contains antiviral compounds.
- Maitake (Grifola frondosa): May help regulate blood sugar.
- Agaricus Blazei: Linked to cardiovascular health.
- Oyster Mushroom (Pleurotus ostreatus): Source of protein and vitamins.
- Porcini (Boletus edulis): Rich in nutrients like selenium.

- Cauliflower Mushroom (Sparassis crispa):
  Supports the immune system.
- Enoki (Flammulina velutipes): Low in
  calories, and high in nutrients.
- Matsutake (Tricholoma matsutake):
  Aromatic and flavorful.
- Shimeji (Hypsizygus tessellatus): Contains
  beta-glucans for immunity.
- Wood Ear (Auricularia auricula-judae): Used
  in traditional medicine.
- Lingzhi (Ganoderma tsugae): Similar
  benefits to Reishi.
- Mesima (Phellinus linteus): Studied for its
  anti-cancer potential.
- Tremella (Tremella fuciformis): Hydrating
  and good for the skin.
- Agaricus Subrufescens: Rich in
  polysaccharides.
- Cordyceps Sinensis: Traditional remedy for
  various ailments.
- Artist's Conk (Ganoderma applanatum):
  Used in folk medicine.
- Poria Mushroom (Poria cocos): Traditional
  in Chinese medicine.
- Red Reishi (Ganoderma resinaceum):
  Variant of Reishi.
- White Button Mushroom (Agaricus
  bisporus): Common in diets.
- Birch Polypore (Piptoporus betulinus):
  Historical medicinal use.

- Velvet Shank (Flammulina velutipes): Contains ergosterol.
- Pioppino Mushroom (Agrocybe aegerita): Good source of fiber.
- Yellow Morel (Morchella esculenta): Culinary and medicinal.
- Pholiota Nameko: Contains immunomodulatory compounds.
- King Trumpet Mushroom (Pleurotus eryngii): Rich in nutrients.
- Golden Oyster Mushroom (Pleurotus citrinopileatus): Antioxidant properties.
- Crimini Mushroom (Agaricus bisporus): Similar to Button Mushroom.
- Black Trumpet Mushroom (Craterellus cornucopioides): Unique flavor.
- Chicken of the Woods (Laetiporus sulphureus): Culinary delight.
- Lentinula edodes (Shiitake): Contains lentinan for immune support.